1. Marie Taglioni, Fanny Elssler, and Fanny Cerrito in
THE THREE GRACES

THE ROMANTIC BALLET

BATSFORD COLOUR BOOKS

2. Fanny Elssler in "The Cracovienne Dance" from
LA GYPSY

The
ROMANTIC BALLET

from Contemporary Prints

*With an Introduction
and Notes on the Plates*

by

SACHEVERELL SITWELL

B. T. BATSFORD LTD
LONDON : NEW YORK : TORONTO : SYDNEY

ACKNOWLEDGMENT

The Author and Publishers wish to express their gratitude to Madame Marie Rambert for lending fourteen original prints from her collection for reproduction in this volume. Also to the Trustees of the British Museum for permission to reproduce one other original print. The remaining subject is in the possession of the Author.

First Published, 1948

Printed in the Netherlands by
L. van LEER & CO.
of London and Amsterdam
for the Publishers
B. T. BATSFORD LTD.
LONDON: 15 North Audley Street, W.1
and Malvern Wells, Worcestershire
NEW YORK: 122 East 55th Street
TORONTO: 480-6 University Avenue
SYDNEY: 156 Castlereagh Street

INTRODUCTION

THE author of this introduction has the good fortune that his working room, by no accidental happening, is a little and untidy shrine dedicated to the dancers of the Romantic Ballet and preserving, therefore, though in the depths of the country, something of the lights of the theatre and the glitter of the town. By only looking round we will find ourselves, in a few moments, in the centre of our subject. Upon the wall, hanging to one side of me as I write these words, there is an exceptional treasure, the original drawing by J. F. Lewis of Pauline Duvernay in her Spanish costume as Florinda in *The Devil on Two Sticks*. Below it, there hangs the beautiful and famous lithograph of Carlotta Grisi in *La Péri*. This is flanked by Miss Fairbrother as Aladdin in *The Forty Thieves,* and by Madame Celeste as *The Arab Boy*. Upon another wall there are Carlotta Grisi and Jules Perrot in *La Polka*. All of these, except the first, are to be found reproduced in the present volume, so that this is no haphazard opening to our selection from these lovely prints. Their brightness of colouring is extraordinary; and it is always difficult to believe that Miss Fairbrother is only a lithograph and not an original water-colour drawing. Miss Fairbrother and Madame Celeste, it is true, were famous beauties more than dancers. Their poses are static; but how gracefully Carlotta Grisi is rising or flying in *La Péri,* and how instinct with the music is *La Polka!* What we would enquire is how faithful are these lithographs as portraits of the dancers, and how accurate are they as portrayals of dancers moving and in action! But, more than all else, since it is not intended for this little book that it should be a mere handlist for collectors, this is our opportunity to write of the dancers and the ballets of a hundred years ago.

A glance at the illustrations reveals the unlikely fact that Marie Taglioni, greatest and most famous of the dancers, is only once represented. She was a very little older than her rivals, a mere five or six years, but this is a considerable time in the life of a dancer, and during the decade of the 'eighteen-forties', which was when the coloured lithographs were at their height of excellence, she was largely away from London and appearing in St. Petersburg. There are beautiful drawings of her by A. E. Chalon, but these belong to the previous decade, and in their original version they are not coloured. In the aggregate, it is easier to judge of Fanny Elssler or Carlotta Grisi, for there is much more material to choose from. But Marie Taglioni, it is clear, was the greatest artist of them all, and it is not possible to write of the Romantic Ballet without paying tribute to *La Sylphide*.

This greatest of female dancers was born and intended for the stage. Her father and grand-father were famous dancers. Her mother was the daughter of a Swedish singer. She was born at Stockholm in 1804, but our concern is less with biographical details, which can be set forth in another place, than with the dancers as artists and as persons. She was one of those artists whom nature has intended, but not forgetting to put natural obstacles in their way in order that they should be conquered and overcome. When she was taking lessons from Coulon in Paris, as a little girl, the other pupils mocked her, saying "Will that little hunchback ever learn to dance?' In the same strain we are told that Paderewski, in Vienna, was advised to give up the career of pianist as his hands were not suited for it. Of Taglioni it was said, 'She was not beautiful, her figure was a little flat, her arms were long'. Our illustration of her by A. E. Chalon, in *The Three Graces,* renders these defects, and they are made the more visible in contrast with the great physical beauty and attraction of her companions, Fanny Elssler and Cerrito, but what is altogether omitted by the painter is her genius. All the artists seem to have abandoned as hopeless the project of representing Taglioni in her elevation. There does not seem to be a single print or drawing in which this has been attempted. For Marie Taglioni had powers of elevation which were altogether phenomenal. Above all she possessed that mysterious faculty of appearing to remain quite still in the air at the apex of her flight, and then to come down slowly in defiance of the laws of gravity, an illusionary gift or secret which has only been shared with her by Vestris and by Nijinski and which, from remarks let drop both by Taglioni and by Nijinski, is a method of breathing. Taglioni is even said to have taught it to her ill-fated pupil, Emma Livry. She was, also, incredible as this may seem, one of the first dancers to appear upon her 'points' so that dancing, in its classical sense, may be said to have begun with her. The white tarlatan dress worn by her in *La Sylphide,* and designed by Eugène Lami, became equally, the traditional dancer's costume in academic ballet. So that, in fact, Taglioni *is* the classical dancer just as much as Grimaldi *is* the clown.

La Sylphide, produced by her father Filippo Taglioni in Paris in 1832, with herself in the title rôle, was the first of the Romantic Ballets and marks an epoch in the history of taste. Marie Taglioni appeared in it with that singular disembodied or ethereal poetry which was her particular genius and which fitted her for that white tarlatan dress and the gauze wings upon her shoulders. It is to be remembered that her portrait in this print is no reminiscence of her youth but a likeness of this great artist when she was about to make her farewell. Chalon, a painter of Huguenot descent born at Geneva in 1781, but who came early in life to London, must have been well acquainted with Taglioni. He was an inveterate attender at the opera and ballet, and made a number of remarkable caricatures of famous singers. Towards the more appealing charms of the dancers he was more favourably disposed, and from the reverence with which his pencil captured *La Sylphide's* features it is to be inferred that he considered Taglioni to be the greatest stage artist of her day. Mr. C. W. Beaumont has remarked that his lithographs show her at different ages, and that in the collection of six, entitled *Souvenir d'Adieu de Marie Taglioni* (1845), all the drawings, it is evident, were not made at the same period. *The Three Graces* is an ideal composition not to be confused with *Le Pas de Quatre,* that famous *pas* or dance in which Taglioni, Grisi, Grahn and Cerrito appeared together upon the stage. In *The Three Graces,* with reticence and forbearance, Chalon has placed Taglioni in her *Sylphide* costume, to one side, and looking away from us, leaving the stage to her younger rivals.

But this lithograph of *The Three Graces* by Chalon which serves as our introduction to the dancers of the Romantic Ballet has other points of interest. The dancers are all shown barefoot. This, as Mr Beaumont points out, is merely a convention, as is the exposed bosom of Cerrito who would never have appeared in this guise in a London theatre. *The Three Graces,* as we have said, is an ideal composition or a souvenir of three great dancers. Fanny Elssler, in the centre, is wearing her Spanish costume as Florinda in *The Devil on Two Sticks,* a rôle later played with much success by Pauline Duvernay at Drury Lane. Cerrito, on the right, is shown in her *Pas de Diane* from *La Jolie Fille de Gand;*[1] but we continue with Fanny Elssler, postponing any further mention of Cerrito for a little time. This most alluring of the ballerinas, for she was that by all accounts compared with the more poetical and ethereal, the more abstract genius of Taglioni, was an Austrian of Viennese origin born at Eisenstadt in 1810, her father having been copyist and valet-secretary to the famous Haydn. Much of her childhood, therefore, was passed 'below' and 'above stairs' in the palace of the Esterhazys for this was one of their great residences down in the Burgenland between Austria and Hungary. In her 'teens Fanny Elssler toured in Italy for five years with Barbaja, the Italian impresario, but her first great success was more delayed than that of Taglioni for it did not take place until she was twenty-six years old when she appeared in Paris in this very part of Florinda in *The Devil on Two Sticks* which had been

---

[1] Let us forbear from translating this, in the modern idiom, as *The Pretty Girl from Ghent.*

3. Fanny Elssler and Jules Perrot in "La Castilliana Bolero" from
LE DÉLIRE D'UN PEINTRE

specially devised for her. The choreography was by Coralli, the old Italian ballet-master who is still famous for *Giselle*. Here, for it cannot be too often quoted, is Théophile Gautier's account of her in the Cachuca in *The Devil on Two Sticks*: 'She comes forward in her pink satin basquine trimmed with wide flounces of black lace; her skirt, weighted at the hem, fits tightly over the hips; her slender waist boldly arches and causes the diamond ornament on her bodice to glitter; her leg, smooth as marble, gleams through the frail mesh of her silk stocking; and her little foot at rest seems but to await the signal of the music. How charming she is with her big comb, the rose behind her ear, her lustrous eyes and sparkling smile . . .!' As to her physical appearance, in general, Gautier has this to say: 'She is tall, supple, and well formed. She has delicate wrists and slim ankles; her legs, elegant and well turned, recall the slender but muscular legs of Diana, the virgin huntress; the knee-caps are well defined, stand out in relief, and make the whole appear beyond reproach . . . Mlle Elssler is endowed with superb hair which falls on each side of her temples, lustrous and glossy as the two wings of a bird; the dark shade of her hair clashes in too southern a manner with her typically German features; it is not the right head for such a body. This peculiarity is very disturbing and affects the harmony of the whole; her eyes, very black, the pupils of which are like two little stars of jet set in a crystal sky, are inconsistent with the nose, which, like the forehead, is German.' Fanny Elssler, in short, allowing for poetical exaggeration, was a dancer of great physical fascination and attraction with a particular aptitude for national dances and rôles of character.

The Devil on Two Sticks, founded on *Le Diable Boiteux* of Le Sage, had peculiar opportunities for Fanny Elssler. There is a delightful flavour even in the old stage directions: 'A magnificent park. On every side are the noble trees and scented flowers of Spain,' and there is a scene in the green-room at the Opera House, Madrid: 'the ballet-master is taking a class when Cleophas and Asmodeus enter.' Coralli, it is to be noted, took the part of an old hairdresser in this scene. There are scenes, too, on the stage of the Opera House, when 'the orchestra strike up the overture and the curtain rises to disclose the auditorium crowded with spectators,' and the corps de ballet dance with their backs to the real audience. Later, in the drawing room of her own house, Florinda dances her Cachuca, and, 'meanwhile, the demon Asmodeus has lifted off the roof so that Cleophas, the student of Alcala, can look down upon his fickle charmer.' In the last scene of all, 'A landscape on the banks of the Manzanares, with the bridge of Toledo spanning its waters,' the stage directions read: 'The *tambour de basque* is heard, the castanets begin their sonorous murmur, the guitar tinkles, and the natives of each province display their local music and dances.' We are in midst of the Romantic Ballet.

Perhaps the most charming portrait that we have of Fanny Elssler, and the most delightful of all the lithographs of dancers, is that of her dancing her Cracovienne in *La Gypsy*. This is drawn and lithographed by J. Bouvier, a Frenchman who worked in London and who is responsible for the most beautiful of the ballet prints, but of whom very little is known. *La Gypsy,* with choreography by Mazilier, afforded Fanny Elssler opportunities as sparkling as her rôle of Florinda in *The Devil on Two Sticks*. This is how she is described by Théophile Gautier: 'She dances in the most coquettish and roguish costume that could be imagined; an officer's tunic sparkling with buttons and a vivandière's skirt, boots with steel spurs, and a black necktie framing a delightful chin—the whole crowned with a triumphant, sprightly little plume, the prettiest you ever saw. It is impossible to describe this dance: it is rhythmic precision mingled with a charming ease, a muscular and bounding agility which cannot be imagined; the metallic clicking of the spurs, a kind of castanets on the heels, emphasizes each step and gives the dance a quality of joyous vivacity which is quite irresistible. This *pas* is encored every evening.' This is exactly how we see Fanny Elssler before us in the lithograph, and we cannot forbear to quote a little from the libretto of *La Gypsy*, for it introduces us to so fascinating a world of make belief. Fanny Elssler, it will be observed in the print, is dancing her Cracovienne in front of Edinburgh Castle, an unlikely setting. But the scene of *La Gypsy* is laid in Scotland. It opens at the castle of Lord Campbell, 'an ardent Royalist', who is celebrating the Restoration of Charles II. 'The clan are assembled and the festival is to begin with a hunt in the mountains,' and we meet Narcisse de Crackentorp, 'Lord Campbell's nephew and a conceited fool.' By the time we reach Act II, 'twelve years have passed,' and the scene shifts to 'a vast tent erected in a street in Edinburgh,' in which Sarah (Fanny Elssler) is resting on a pile of tiger skins. It is in the following scene that she dances her Cracovienne 'in the market place at the great fair of Edinburgh'.

Another lithograph by J. Bouvier, not reproduced here, depicts Fanny Elssler as Lauretta in *La Tarentule*, another ballet by Jean Coralli. Her tarentella was performed to the music of *La Danza*, the popular Neapolitan air by Rossini which is known to living audiences from *La Boutique Fantasque*. In the meantime Luigi, her lover, a young peasant, has been bitten by the tarantula spider, and 'restrained with difficulty by his companions, crosses the stage with spasmodic *cabrioles*, and soon falls exhausted into the arms of Lauretta and her mother'. After her dashing and exciting performance to the music of *La Danza* Fanny Elssler returned upon the stage in order to mime the misfortune that had befallen her lover by 'a combination of trembling and dancing that were quite indescribable'. Later, she is bitten herself by the spider, or pretends to be, feigns death, and only descends from the bier at her own funeral procession in order to be united with her lover. Fanny Elssler, it is clear, excelled in Spanish, Polish, Neapolitan dances, as in the print of her in *La Castilliana Bolero* from *Le Délire d'un Peintre*, by J Bouvier, in which she is to be seen with Jules Perrot. She must have been of entirely different temperament from Taglioni, more vital and human, less, probably, of an artist, with little or nothing of poetry in her presentation.

Carlotta Grisi, the original *Giselle*, and third in order of the ballerinas of the Romantic Ballet, was a Northern Italian born at Visinada, a hunting lodge of the Habsburg's, near Mantua, in 1819. Giulia Grisi, the singer, was her cousin and she showed considerable promise, herself, as an operatic singer, but by the time she was fourteen years old she was touring Italy with a company of dancers, meeting in this way with Jules Perrot at Naples before she was twenty years old.

Théophile Gautier, another victim of her charms, wrote of her that 'she reminds one of a tea-rose about to bloom. She has a well-proportioned body which, although slender and light, has nothing of that attenuated anatomy which so often makes dancers resemble racehorses in training—all bone and muscle'. It is curious, therefore, that Chorley, the English critic, should, also, have remarked of Grisi, that 'she looked shy and young and fresh. There was something of the briar rose in her beauty'. The print of her by J. Brandard in *Giselle* seems to exactly capture that image or resemblance. *Giselle*, as we have said, was the most famous of her rôles, devised for her specially by Théophile Gautier who was her admirer. In the lithograph of Carlotta Grisi in *La Péri*, also by J. Brandard, here reproduced, this dewy youthfulness and freshness appear again, and once more in a rôle devised for her by Gautier.

Esmeralda, a ballet by Jules Perrot based upon Victor Hugo's *Nôtre Dame de Paris*, and first produced in London at Her Majesty's theatre in 1844, was after *La Péri* and *Giselle* the most famous rôle of Grisi. This old ballet, we are told, is still occasionally performed in Russia. In the print, again by J. Bouvier, we have what must be an excellent likeness of the two great dancers, Grisi and Perrot. Already in *Giselle*, which was first given two years before, Perrot composed most of the individual dances which were performed by Grisi, and it is melancholy to reflect that the shadow of these, for after the passage of more than a hundred years they can be little more than an echo or reflection of the original, is all that is left to us of the greatest male dancer and choreographer of his time. Jules Perrot, there can be little doubt, was the foremost male dancer between Vestris and Nijinski. As a youth he had toured for several years as an acrobat with a travelling circus, an adventure that fell to the lot of other famous actors

4

4. Carlotta Grisi in *LA PERI*

5. Carlotta Grisi and Jules Perrot in *LA ESMERALDA*

6. Carlotta Grisi in *GISELLE*

7. Carlotta Grisi and Jules Perrot in *LA POLKA*

and dancers, for instance, Deburau and Edmund Kean. This must be the most valuable school of experience for the stage, not only for feats of agility but for rapid improvisation and for mime. Gautier wrote of Perrot: 'From the waist upwards he has the proportions of a tenor, there is no need to say more; but, from the waist downwards, he is delightful to look at . . . Let us add that Perrot, in a costume by Gavarni, has nothing of that feeble and inane manner which, as a rule, makes male dancers so tiresome; his success was assured before he made a single step even.' It is to be noted that in the lithograph of Grisi and Perrot in *Esmeralda* the male dancer appears as a youthful figure though Perrot at that time was close on forty-five years old. The portrait of Grisi is unusually charming. Not only must it be a good likeness of her features but it gives us the style and manner of her dancing. Perrot, unfortunately, is only kneeling. We do not see him in action in this lithograph.

But, in *La Polka*, Perrot and Grisi are both dancing. They are dressed in red and white, the national colours of Poland, and he wears the czapska or Polish dancer's cap. The white skirt of Grisi, and her cap and military tunic, suggest the costume of a vivandière. Perrot wears spurs upon his red boots, while Grisi, as can be seen by comparing the prints, has the same little metal contrivance upon the heels of her red shoes as were worn by Elssler for her Cracovienne from *La Gypsy*. This is again, in fact, 'the metallic clicking of the spurs, a kind of castanets on the heels', which Gautier describes. Grisi, it was noticed by various writers, appeared to combine in herself some of the qualities of both Marie Taglioni and Fanny Elssler, and in this instance she appears to have set herself out, deliberately, to rival Fanny Elssler. This dance, in semi-military costume, was in the Elssler manner. The backcloth, in the lithograph, depicts what was to be intended a Polish town, though, by a scene painter's mistake, the churches with their golden onion domes are Russian Orthodox, not Polish Catholic in style. Nothing certain is known as to the derivation of *La Polka*. It was probably a single dance taken from a divertissement by Perrot, and from a Ballet Music Title we know that the music was by Pugni.

The three female dancers of whom we have written were the immortals of the Romantic Ballet. Perrot is the only male dancer whom we have met so far. This is because all the emphasis in the Romantic Ballet was upon the ballerina. The male was the partner; he was used more often for comic or semi-comical rôles, an old father, a pedantic doctor, a lawyer—and of course the choreographer was a male dancer; but it was only the outstanding abilities of Jules Perrot as mime and dancer that led to his portrait being left to us in *Esmeralda* and *La Polka*. In general, and after calculation, it may be said that male dancers only appear in one out of five of the lithographs of dancers. After looking at the prints we get a definite impression of Marie Taglioni, of Fanny Elssler, of Carlotta Grisi, but our mental image of Perrot remains but shadowy and incomplete. There are no prints of Perrot alone.

Fanny Cerrito, the next of the ballerinas, is preserved to us in a great number of portraits. She was born at Naples in 1821 and made her début at the San Carlo. By the time she was twenty years old she had appeared in London at Her Majesty's theatre. She was, indeed, a particular favourite in London. Her movement and action as a dancer are indicated in the words of the critic of *The Times* who refers to her 'favourite rotatory movement', and to 'the wonderful flying leaps and revolving bounds of Cerrito . . . who by her very smallness of stature seems fitted by nature for another style of dancing'. The print of her in *Ondine,* a ballet by Perrot first produced in London, must be a faithful portrait of her charms. This lithograph, it is to be noted, though published in London, is 'after a drawing by Numa Blanc', a painter whom I have been unable to identify unless he is the same Numa of the fashion plates who is eulogized by Baudelaire in 'Le Peintre de la Vie Moderne'. It may yield us, too, some little indication of the worth of the scene painter W. Grieve, who was famous for his scenery for Oriental plays and for the pantomimes at Drury Lane and Covent Garden, for it was W. Grieve who painted the scenery for *Ondine*. The same choreographer, Jules Perrot, and the same scene painter produced the ballet *Alma ou la Fille de Feu*, in which Cerrito played one of her most famous rôles, and of which a lithograph by Bouvier is the souvenir. She is dancing with a tambourine and about to execute one of 'her favourite rotatory movements'. We see her again in *La Lituana*, obviously, from her costume, a mazurka or some other national dance, another proof of which is her left hand resting on her hip. We have a portrait of her, again by Bouvier, in *La Redowa Polka*. In this lithograph she is dancing with Arthur Saint-Léon, her husband, in the latter's ballet *La Vivandière*. The Redowa, or Redowotchka, was a waltz, danced back to back, and requiring some particular rhythms in the music. There is a Redowa in Offenbach's *La Vie Parisienne* (1867), but this mid-Victorian waltz seems to have fallen into obscurity since then. In the print, Cerrito, in her vivandière's apron, shows in the words of *The Times* critic that the Redowa was 'full of life, character and fun . . . carried on during a pretty sort of stamping movement. Now the pair seem infinitely pleased with each other; now they seem determined to try each other's temper, and the ill-humour of the one is always vanquished by the growing kindness of the other'. The Redowa, in fact, was a character dance partaking of the Styrienne and the Zapateado. The pair to this lithograph, 'by and after' J. Bouvier, and published in the same year, 1844, gives us Fanny Cerrito in another scene from *La Vivandière*, standing on a rustic bridge of wooden planks waving a flag in one hand, wearing a military cap, a Hussar's slung jacket, and with her vivandière's wooden keg or barrel of brandy upon her hip. This charmingly old-fashioned little ballet, in one act, with its echoes of *La Fille du Regiment*, might well be intolerable to a modern audience but the true field of ballet subjects, as that of lyric poetry, is set and limited and the theme of a vivandière, like that of the doll become alive in *Coppélia* or *La Boutique Fantasque*, had such opportunities, choreographically, that it could not be neglected. We await a 'modern' ballet with, for heroine, the stewardess in an air-liner!

Another of the dancers of the Romantic Ballet, and the exact contemporary of Cerrito, was Lucile Grahn, a Dane, who was born at Copenhagen. Of the famous *Pas de Quatre*, danced by Taglioni, Grisi, Cerrito and Grahn, *The Times* critic has this to say of her, after his eulogy of Taglioni: 'Lucile Grahn, a disciple of the same school . . . the dancer who has followed the same track' (as Taglioni); while of *Le Jugement de Paris*, produced in London the next year, 1846, he again remarks: 'though the styles of Taglioni and Lucile Grahn, at first sight would seem to be identical,' from all of which it is to be inferred that Grahn was not of the school of Grisi or Cerrito. In the print of her in *Eoline ou la Dryade*, a ballet of Perrot's, she is, certainly, in something of the attitude of Taglioni. In *Catarina ou la Fille du Bandit*, another ballet of Perrot's, Grahn appeared in quite another character in her famous *Pas Stratégique*. There are beautiful prints and music titles of her in this rôle by J. Brandard. She danced, musket on shoulder, in a blue skirt, military jacket, and peaked Calabrian hat, at the head of female bandits dressed in bright red, and under her command they mimed the different phases of guerrilla warfare: 'First, general merriment and preparations for battle; then the attempt to surprise the enemy; the general attack; the defence; and retreat.' There are beautiful music titles, too, also by Brandard, of Lucile Grahn and Perrot in the Valse Silésienne and the Mazurka d'Extase from *Eoline*, and indeed, from Brandard's lithographs a very good idea can be formed of Grahn's personal appearance and her dancing. This last of the great dancers, survived into recent times, only dying at Munich in 1907.

The remaining lithographs illustrated in this present book, and which as works of art are in no way inferior to those that have preceded them, have for their subject lesser dancers. Here is Flora Fabbri in *The Devil to Pay* (*Le Diable à Quatre*), a ballet by Mazilier, with a Polish setting and music by Adolphe Adam which might be worth reviving. The fame of this ballerina lay in her rendering of national dances. Her rôle in this ballet had been created by Carlotta Grisi and it called for the execution of Krakoviaks and Mazurkas, indeed the title rôle is Mazourka, who is the wife of Mazourki, a basket maker, while the last scene in *Le Diable à Quatre*, concluding with a national dance, takes place in a 'splendid gallery forming a greenhouse fitted with the rarest flowers'.

One of the most delightful of all the ballet prints in style and colouring is that of Marie Guy Stéphan in *Las Boleras de Cadiz*. As a lithograph of a dancer in Spanish costume this is to be compared with the print of Pauline Duvernay in the Cachuca from *The Devil on Two Sticks*, the only ballet print by that considerable minor artist, J. F. Lewis. The 'pink satin basquine trimmed with wide flounces of black lace', the skirt 'weighted at the hem, and fitting tightly over the hips', as worn by the ravishingly beautiful Pauline Duvernay, contrasts with the yellow basquine trimmed with a wide black lace flounce worn by Marie Guy Stéphan. They are, both of them, Spanish dresses closely akin to those I saw worn this year at the Feria of Seville; and I was reminded of them when I called at the premises of the most famous dressmaker in Seville and saw the dresses of the Spanish dancers hanging on the walls, a little different in style, of course, from those worn at the Feria which are influenced by Flamenco fashions, and are larger; they are, indeed, crinoline without the whale bones, and are, more usually, of white organdie spotted with red or green. But, nevertheless, it was a reminiscence and one could have fancied oneself for a few moments admitted into the dressing room of Fanny Elssler, of Pauline Duvernay, or of Marie Guy Stéphan. In the lithograph she has the castanets in her hands; we admire her little black sleeves, the rose in her hair, her Spanish coiffure, and the thin and pointed black bodice which accentuates her waist; and what does it matter if the scene painter at Her Majesty's theatre (we copy from the print) has in mistake given us Venice and not Seville for the background, as we see from the typical Venetian chimney, the wooden shutters to the houses, the Gothic balcony, and the church front which so closely resembles that of the Scuola di San Marco, next door to Santi Giovanni e Paolo, that we crane our necks for a glimpse of the statue of Colleoni, and find ourselves listening for the cry of the gondolier as the prow of his long thin black craft comes round the corner into the stagnant waters of the Rio dei Mendicanti! The charming ambiguities of the contemporary scene painter are further illustrated in another print of Marie Guy Stéphan, this time by Bouvier, in which she is depicted in La Cracovienne from *Une Soirée de Carnaval, divertissement de Monsr. Perrot*, a Polish dance, therefore, but we notice that she is standing, or rather dancing, below a Moorish archway, and that the artist has been anything but flattering to her features. She is not to be recognized, in fact, as the dancer of *Las Boleras de Cadiz*.

Nevertheless, our choice of ballet prints ends upon a note of personal beauty rather than technical accomplishment. The last instance is the portrait of Louise Fairbrother as Aladdin in *The Forty Thieves*, a pantomime. It is a lithograph by Brandard after a drawing by J. W. Child, the same artist who drew the portrait of Flora Fabbri in *The Devil to Pay*, but next to nothing is known of him except that he was born in 1778 and died in 1862, and was in request for his portraits or miniatures of popular stage favourites. At the Garrick Club one entire wall of a corridor is nearly covered with a collection of drawings by this painter of Charles Mathews in his different rôles. Louise Fairbrother is quite enchanting in her Albanian dress. Never again, can the principal boy of a pantomime have been made immortal with her false imperial and moustache. Another print, again by J. W. Childe and Brandard, depicts this beautiful actress as Eglantine in *Valentine and Orson*, a lithograph of less seductive colouring, but her costume as an Amazon could be the original of the spangled print of 'penny plain and tuppence coloured'! Her breastplate, short ballet skirt, and the grieves upon her legs, glitter with sequins and little bits of coloured paste or glass. Louise Fairbrother, it is not difficult to guess, had great personal charms, and in her travesty, whether as Amazon or principal boy, won the heart of the Duke of Cambridge, Commander in Chief of the British Army during the half-century between the Crimean and Boer Wars, and became his morganatic wife.

Madame Celeste, a more serious problem as actress and dancer, is the subject of the penultimate illustration. Celine Celeste, a Parisian, made her début in New York at a very early age, coming, afterwards, to London. We see her, in the print, in her famous rôle of *The Dumb Arab Boy,* from *The French Spy,* 'a piece written especially to show her talent,' and put on at the Queen's Theatre in 1831, before she was twenty years old, but the lithograph dates from 1838 when this popular piece must have been revived; so popular was it, indeed, that we are told there is still a public house somewhere in Hampstead called *The Arab Boy.* The artist was W. Drummond, as unknown to fame as James Warren Childe who drew the pair of portraits of Louise Fairbrother. Celine Celeste toured in Italy, Germany, Spain and France, and made a fortune in America, but was most at home in London. The ballet prints of her are several in number, including one by J. W. Childe in which she appears in Red Indian dress, musket on shoulder, in the curiously named rôle of Miami in *Green Bushes.* Another of her famous rôles was in *The Maid of Cashmere,* of which there are prints, and there is a lithograph of her by A. E. Chalon as Madeline in *St. Mary's Eve,* which was her first speaking part, for Celeste was not content with dancing. But she appeared, too, in burlesques of *Giselle* and of *The Devil on Two Sticks,* a form of travesty to which the London stage was more than partial and for which, as we shall see, it developed peculiar and special talents. *Taming a Tartar, or Magic and Mazurkaphobia* was the title of one of these. The costumes were 'of the Bohemian character', and it included the 'real Bohemian Polka' danced by Madame Celeste, who played the wife of the basket-maker, or, in other words, this was a travesty, not of *Le Diable Boiteux* (*The Devil on Two Sticks*), but of *Le Diable à Quatre,* in which Mazourka, the wife of the basket-maker, was played by Carlotta Grisi. In the Pas de Fascination, according to *The Times,* Madame Celeste 'quits the burlesque and becomes a dancer of a high order'. Later on in her career, in the 1850's, she introduced a new character into pantomime, that of Harlequin in travesty, or Harlequin à la Watteau, or, as it was called in the pantomime programmes, Harlequina. Into those realms of magic we have, alas, no space to follow her, but have to be contented with *The Dumb Arab Boy.* It is one of the most beautiful of all the prints of dancers, and we make it the occasion for some concluding words on the dancers and lithographs of the Romantic Ballet.

The 'thirties and 'forties were not only the golden age of Romantic Ballet; they were, as well, the golden age of pantomime, a parallel development which explains the excellence of both. For the English pantomimists were noted dancers and played dual rôles in pantomime and ballet. They would appear at Drury Lane in the Christmas pantomime, or Easter spectacle, and for the summer season at Her Majesty's Theatre or the Royal Italian Opera, Covent Garden. The clowns, Tom Matthews, George Wieland, Dicky Flexmore, were something more than clowns. They were eccentric dancers of genius, with ability either to burlesque, or to play in straight rôles with the greatest dancers of the Romantic Ballet. Dicky Flexmore, for instance, was 'especially noted for his close and natural imitation of leading dancers of the day, such as Perrot, Carlotta Grisi and Cerrito'. In 1848 he revived *Esmeralda,* playing the rôle of Gringoire, the part created by Perrot, the greatest male dancer of the age. There is a ballet print of Flexmore in this part with his wife, Mme Auriol, who was the daughter of a French clown. Tom Matthews, another clown and dancer, was famed for his parody of Fanny Elssler and Pauline Duvernay in their *Cachuca* in *The Devil on Two Sticks.* This was even given in the actual ballet with Duvernay as Florinda and Tom Matthews as a comic dancer; then Matthews, as clown in the pantomime that followed, burlesqued Duvernay in her *Cachuca.* George Wieland, the imp or sprite, for that was his part in pantomime, used to play Asmodeus in *The Devil on Two Sticks. The Times* wrote of him: 'Wieland, who, of course, plays Asmodeus, is perfectly exhaustless in invention. The gestures into which he throws himself, with the assistance of his crutches, his extravagant outbursts of passion, are chefs d'œuvres of grotesque art. Wieland must think in arabesque.'

8. Fanny Cerrito in *LA LITUANA*

9. Fanny Cerrito in *ONDINE*

10. Fanny Cerrito in *ALMA*

11.   Fanny Cerrito and Saint-Léon in *LA REDOWA POLKA*

12.   Lucile Grahn in *EOLINE OU LA DRYADE*

13. Marie Guy Stephan in *LAS BOLERAS DE CADIZ*

Later, Wieland played in *La Fille du Danube*, in *La Sylphide*, in a burlesque of *Le Diable Amoureux*, and in *Alma, ou la Fille du Feu*. Of the women dancers, generally columbines in pantomime, it is read, so often, that they had 'studied, in Paris, of the best masters'. As to the popularity of ballet in London it is to be noted that there were no fewer than four separate parodies of *The Devil on Two Sticks* produced in the one year, 1845. Furthermore, the same scene painters, W. Grieve, the Marshalls, etc., who were the glory of English pantomime, often painted the scenery for the ballets produced in London under the management of Benjamin Lumley, and it is this impresario who was responsible for the success in this country of the Romantic Ballet, being the lessee of Her Majesty's Theatre, and producing ballets from 1842 to 1858. It was Lumley who made the contracts with the great dancers and the choreographers, and it is his name that must be associated with the rage in London for the Romantic Ballet.[1]

The ballet prints, moreover, are in greater part of London origin. This may have been due to some special facilities given by Lumley, or to his encouragement, for the artists in question must have been again and again to the theatre, and been allowed behind the stage. There were two firms of print-sellers who specialized in these lithographs, Fores, and T. McLean; while, of the ballet artists, Brandard worked for the former firm, and Bouvier for McLean. John Brandard, who was also the chief designer of the Ballet Music Titles, was born at Birmingham in 1812, and became a commercial lithographer with a wide range of output producing lithographs upon every conceivable subject, including a series of early railway trains. But Brandard, who is, perhaps, not fairly represented in the present series, was of an astonishing degree of accuracy where dancing was concerned. In his Ballet Music Titles, no one of which is illustrated here, the impression given is that of an actual sketch taken from the stalls, and the effect is so momentary that the figures, only, are given and no account is taken of the scene. The lithographs by Bouvier, in contrast, are more finished and more formal, and care has been taken to present a completed picture and to give the painted scene. There are several of Bouvier's prints from which a good idea can be formed of the scenery of W. Grieve, the scene painter to whom we have referred. In Fanny Elssler in her Cracovienne from *La Gypsy* we get what must have been the actual backcloth with the view of Edinburgh Castle, and the same thing may be said of the lithographs of Carlotta Grisi in *Esmeralda* and in *La Polka*.

---

[1] Under the management of Benjamin Lumley there were produced at Her Majesty's Theatre seven ballets by Paul Taglioni, one by Saint Léon, one by Fanny Cerrito, and ten by Jules Perrot, and many operas by Donizetti and by Verdi.

NOTES TO BALLET PRINTS

1. *The Three Graces*. TAGLIONI, ELSSLER and CERRITO. A lithograph from a drawing by A. E. Chalon.

This, one of the most beautiful of all the ballet prints, must not be confused with *Le Pas de Quatre*, also by Chalon (and there is a music cover, too, by Brandard). It is an ideal composition, not an actual *pas*, and shows Taglioni, on the right hand, as *La Sylphide*, Elssler in the centre as Florinda in *The Devil on Two Sticks*, and Cerrito, on the left hand, in the *Pas de Diane* from *La Jolie Fille de Gand*. The print depicts the dancers with bare feet, a convention that is carried still further in the exposed bosom of Cerrito. This must be an excellent portrait of Elssler in the Spanish dancer's dress in which she performed her celebrated Cachuca.

2. FANNY ELSSLER in *The Cracovienne Dance* from *La Gypsy*. A lithograph by, and after, J. Bouvier, published by McLean, 1839.

Fanny Elssler dances the Cracovienne in the market place below Edinburgh Castle. She is dancing, as described by Gautier, in an officer's tunic sparkling with buttons, a vivandière's skirt, and red boots with steel spurs, 'a kind of castanets', Gautier continues, 'upon her heels', and he mentions 'the metallic clicking of her spurs'. He admired, also, 'the triumphant, sprightly little plume in her officer's cap', and calls it 'the most roguish costume that could be imagined'. We may admire, for ourselves, her two long pigtails and her blue skirt, and conclude that this is one of the most alluring of all the prints of dancers.

La Gypsy, with its Scottish setting, was a ballet by Mazilier. Another favourite rôle of Elssler was that of Laurette in *La Tarentule*, by Coralli, but upon her tours in Europe and in the United States she appeared in divertissements and national dances, often arranged for her by Perrot.

3. FANNY ELSSLER and JULES PERROT in *La Castilliana Bolero* from the ballet *Le Délire d'un Peintre*. A lithograph by, and after, J. Bouvier, published by McLean, 1843.

Fanny Elssler, of Viennese extraction, born at Eisenstadt in 1810, appeared in Paris in 1836 in *Le Diable Boiteux* (*The Devil on Two Sticks*), a ballet by Coralli. Thenceforward, she was a European and an American sensation. Elssler was a dancer of great personal fire and beauty, as can be judged from the accounts by Théophile Gautier, particularly renowned for her Spanish dances such as the Cachuca, and for her dancing of the Tarantella in *La Tarentule*.

4. CARLOTTA GRISI in *La Péri*. A lithograph by, and after, J. Brandard, published by Fores, 1844.

This is the most finished of all the prints by Brandard (1812–1863), a Birmingham artist who practised commercial lithography upon a large scale, designed several ballet prints, and was responsible for the greater number of ballet music titles. *La Péri*, another ballet by Coralli, had a book by Gautier and was devised, like *Giselle*, especially for Grisi. The flying, floating effect of her elevation is beautifully rendered. In the autumn of the same year (1843) in which *La Péri* was produced in Paris, it was given at the Theatre Royal, Drury Lane, where Grisi repeated her triumphs, her partner being Lucien Petipa, brother of the more famous Marius Petipa.

5. CARLOTTA GRISI and JULES PERROT in *Esmeralda*. A lithograph by, and after J. Bouvier, published by McLean, 1844.

La Esmeralda, which is still performed in Russia, was a ballet by Perrot based upon Victor Hugo's *Notre Dame de Paris*. Perrot is shown in his famous rôle of Gringoire, and it is perhaps worthy of note that having been born in 1800 he was at this time forty-four years of age, far older than he appears in the lithograph. He had met Carlotta Grisi, when she was dancing at the San Carlo theatre as a young girl of twenty. This lithograph is a beautiful souvenir of Grisi, third and last of the great ballerinas of the Romantic Ballet, and of Perrot, one of the greatest of choreographers, and the·most remarkable male dancer between the time of Vestris and Nijinski.

6. CARLOTTA GRISI in *Giselle*. A lithograph by, and after, J. Brandard, published by Fores.
Carlotta Grisi created the rôle of *Giselle* in 1841. This being the only one of the old ballets which is still familiar to a modern audience, it is scarcely necessary to reiterate that the ballet is by Coralli, the book by Théophile Gautier, and the music by Adolphe Adam.

7. CARLOTTA GRISI and JULES PERROT in *La Polka*. A lithograph by, and after, J. Bouvier, published by McLean, 1844.
The same pair of dancers, Grisi and Perrot, in a *Polka* performed at Her Majesty's Theatre, the scene of so many of the London triumphs of the Romantic Ballet. Grisi, it has been remarked before, seems to have combined in herself something of the talents of a Taglioni and an Elssler. *Giselle* could with some truth be called a Taglioni rôle, but, in her *polka* danced with Perrot, Grisi was rivalling the smolenska, the cachuca, the zapateado of Elssler. The Polka, said to have been invented by a Bohemian housemaid living in Vienna, had just become a fashionable dance. Johann Strauss wrote a number of Polkas which are not less brilliant and full of melody than his Waltzes, and we should mention too, the Polkas of the Czech composer, Smetana. It is with such knowledge in mind that we see Grisi and Perrot just at the start of their vertiginous dance. Grisi is wearing red boots resembling those worn by Elssler in her *Cracovienne* (plate 3), and designed for the same effect, the metallic clicking of the spurs. At Erzeksànad in Hungary this very effect occurs, so to speak, in nature, for we are told that the peasant dancers have a little gadget formed of metal plates in the heels of their red top-boots to make a clicking noise as they walk or dance, and that these are called 'musical heels' in the local dialect of Hungarian. The lithographs of *La Cracovienne* and *La Polka*, both by Bouvier, are probably the finest prints of the Romantic Ballet. States of *La Polka* vary considerably; and there are copies with the tunic and bodice of the dancers coloured blue. But red and white, it may be noted, are the colours of Poland.

8. FANNY CERRITO in *La Lituana*. A lithograph by, and after, J. Bouvier, published by McLean, 1840.
Fanny Cerrito, a Neapolitan dancer, born 1821, made her début at the San Carlo and came to London in 1840. She was married to the dancer and choreographer Saint-Léon. The Lituana, as we can tell from the costume and from Cerrito's attitude, was a Polish dance, a kind of mazurka or smolenska. This is implied, too, in her fur-trimmed jacket. Yet in the background there appear to be the mosques and minarets of Istanbul!

9. FANNY CERRITO in *Ondine*. A lithograph by C. Graf after a drawing by Numa Blanc, published by John Mitchell, 1843.
This print, though published in London, appears to be of French origin. *Ondine* was a ballet by Perrot, first produced at Her Majesty's Theatre with scenery by W. Grieve, the great English scene painter of the day, who painted many of the wonderful scenes in pantomimes, and this print is of particular interest because it may convey some impression of Grieve's costumes and scenic effects. Cerrito, it will be noticed, appears again as in *The Three Graces*, with an exposed bosom though the truth of this may be considered doubtful in Victorian London. Cerrito was short and round, but of decided charms, and was possessed of great technical abilities as a dancer. Always a favourite in London she did not make her Paris début till 1847. Two years before this she danced in the famous *Pas de Quatre* with Lucile Grahn,

Grisi and Taglioni. Her successes were mostly in her husband's ballets, *La Vivandière*, *La Fille deMarbre*, *Stella* and *Le Violon du Diable*.

10. FANNY CERRITO in *Alma*. A lithograph by, and after, J. Bouvier, published by McLean, 1842.

Alma, ou la Fille du Feu, a ballet by Perrot, again with scenery by W. Grieve, had its premiére at Her Majesty's, and was a favourite rôle with Cerrito, who was always applauded in her *Pas de Fascination*, and for her 'brilliant revolving steps' in the *Pas de Trois* of the third act.

11. FANNY CERRITO and SAINT-LÉON in *La Redowa Polka*. A lithograph by, and after, J. Bouvier, published by McLean, 1844.

A redowa was a kind of waltz danced back to back, a character dance, introduced for the first time by Saint-Léon into his ballet *La Vivandière*, though there is a redowa in Meyerbeer's *La Prophéte*, 1841. Saint-Léon was a violinist as well as dancer. He produced *Le Violon du Diable* especially in order to exhibit himself in this capacity, and would seem to have been a considerable virtuoso, or to have had the mimetic talent to give that impression, for in an Almanac de Cour of the Duchy of Parma for 1844, beautifully printed by the firm of Bodoni, his name appears as chamber virtuoso to the Archduchess Marie-Louise in succession to Baron Niccolo Paganini. Saint-Léon produced the famous old fairy tale ballet of *The Hump-Backed Horse* at St Petersburg in 1864, this being the first ballet to be based upon a Russian theme and to have Russian dances incorporated in it. He also collaborated with Nuitter in the books of both *La Source* and *Coppélia* and may, therefore, have influenced Delibes.

12. LUCILE GRAHN in *Éoline, ou la Dryade*. A lithograph by Edward Morton after a drawing by S. M. Joy, published by Mitchell, 1845.

Eoline was a ballet by Perrot produced in London. In the print we see Lucile Grahn, the Danish ballerina, and fourth member of the famous *Pas de Quatre*, as the dryad. The sensation of Eoline, however, was the *Mazurka d'Extase*, which Lucile Grahn danced with Perrot as Rubezahl, a gnome or demon. Two of the finest of Brandard's ballet music titles depict Grahn and Perrot in this dance. The gnome makes Eoline dance with him against her will, and with Brandard for eye-witness, we may follow in the words of the critic of *The Times*, 'the despair with which she falls into the arms of her tormentor'.

13. MARIE GUY STÉPHAN in *Las Boleras de Cadiz*. A lithograph by C. G. Lynch after a drawing by J. H. Lynch, published by William Spooner, 1844.

Marie Guy Stéphan in one of the Spanish dances which have their original association with Fanny Elssler (*La Castilliana Bolero*, *El Jaleo de Jerez* or *El Zapateado*). Marie Guy Stéphan was a minor, but charming dancer, though not flattered in a lithograph of her by Bouvier in a *Cracovienne;* but *Las Boleras de Cadiz* is the most beautiful in colour of all the prints of Spanish dances. Her pink or yellow skirt is but rivalled by the pink satin and black lace of Pauline Duvernay as Florinda in *The Devil on Two Sticks,* a lithograph by J. F. Lewis.

14. FLORA FABBRI in *The Devil to Pay* (Le Diable à Quatre). A lithograph by J. Brandard, after a drawing by J. W. Child, published by Fores, 1846.

Le Diable à Quatre, a ballet by Mazilier, was originally produced with Carlotta Grisi in the part of Mazourka. Flora Fabbri played the rôle in the London production.

15. MADAME CELESTE as *The Arab Boy*. A lithograph by, and after, William Drummond, published by McLean, 1838.

The celebrated French dancer and actress in her most famous rôle.

16. MISS FAIRBROTHER as *Aladdin* in *The Forty Thieves*. A lithograph by J. Brandard, after a drawing by J. W. Childe, published by Fores, 1845.

Miss Fairbrother, 'the principal boy' of pantomime *in excelsis*, left the stage to become the morganatic wife of F.M. the Duke of Cambridge.

14. Flora Fabbri in *LE DIABLE A QUATRE*

15. Madame Celeste as *THE ARAB BOY*

16. Miss Fairbrother as "Aladdin" in *THE FORTY THIEVES*